5 – They say

6 – Changeling

8 – You're never too old to be young

10 – You wrote my love on a toilet wall in Alloa

11 – Taps aff

12 – In concert

14 – Scream if you wantae go faster

15 – Teacups

16 – Palette

18 – Mountain Rescue

19 – Where my roots lie

22 – Bonfires

23 – Ghost apples

24 – Big John, Dhanakosa, 2014

26 – Her slow-beating heart

28 – Flight

29 – Over the edge of blue

ego

They say

we stood, all the better to sight danger.
That a girl's footprints, fossilised
on a prehistoric shore, were left
while she combed for shellfish.

Why not assume we rose
to gaze all the closer to the stars?
Pressed our toes into sand
while dancing with waves?

Because there's danger
too in stargazing. Nourishment
in dancing with tides.

Changeling

She was born one morning
as a nervous tic in my right eyelid.
I raised my hand to still her
and she emerged from my tear duct,
waved and twinkled a smile.

I, entranced, shook her hand
with my pinkie tip.
That day, she rode the rim
of my glasses.

That night, she lay on my earlobe
and whispered of all the things
we might someday do.
I fed her with my dreams
and she grew.

I awoke, a weight pressing.
She sat on my chest,
heavy with all the things
I might have done.
Below her, I could not move.
Her face was mine, my face now hers,
glowing with potential.

I shrank
to nearly nothing
and she leaned down,
butterfly-kissed me,
spidery lashes a flutter,
she swept me
into her left eye.

I tug, occasionally,
on her eyelid.

You're never too old to be young

She arrived nearly new.
Just a few scuff marks on her chassis.
Very little sagging in her upholstery.
Flawless structure.
She had promise.

She spoke to the first of us, a doctor.
I'm wishing...
I'm hoping...
I'm dreaming...
Make me happy.

Our dermatologist softened her with a gift:
peachy skin, delectably touchable.

The stylist gave her hair the colour of
witching-hour. Spellbinding. Pink cheeks,
a permanent blush, lips that tasted of apple.
Buffed her eyes to a tear-spilling shine.

The dresser fitted her in heels so high she couldn't
run. Filed her nails down so they were too blunt
to scratch. And squeezed her into a corset
too tight to take a breath in.
Not that she often needed to.

The sound engineer gave her a nightingale
trill of a voice, a playlist ready to go.

Then the programmer: love, honour and obey.
Whistle while you work.

We stood back and observed her,
pristine in her glass case.
Heigh-ho, we said.
All done.
She really is the fairest of them all.
One day her prince will come.

The last of us matched her up,
his algorithms twinkling their magic,
and a charming man appeared,
pressed his lips to hers,
the signal to turn her on.

You wrote my love on a toilet wall in Alloa

Is there something to be said for evolving beyond the tyranny of proper nouns?

Let's see. Pull up a roster of passengers. It won't matter who gives answers or asks the questions. Just that they're asked and given. With the arrival of dawn, nobody will get up unless they want to. No clouds will chafe into the static build-up of thunder. Here lie... cookies and carbon footprints. We'll know each other by the sounds of our voices, bleating in a field. There are no names on cave paintings. Only handprints. Socials will be absent of selfies. It won't matter which man discovered the G-spot, just that it was enjoyed. We love so that we can exist beyond ourselves. You vibrate out into the same energy you came from. A democracy of soundwaves weaving. In a vacuum nobody can hear you scream. Old names will fade, relationships smear to green. Instead we'll memorialise on our bodies the kisses others leave, watermark lines around our bruises, glorify our scars. I wish there were nothing between us. Open the cracks in walls and let each other flow through. There are no secrets here. It won't matter who you address letters to. Art will become fluid again and drip down the walls. Nobody will take us in vain. We'll become the glint of light on water. A missing cog in the machine. A brick-of-brack in a box of lost property. A flower by any other name still smells the same. The squiggles formerly known as people. Maybe it's time to become a hermit. The rattle of seeds in a poppy husk. Let go. Smile back at the I you were a moment ago. Imagine who we'd be if we didn't have to be anyone. It's amazing what we do when we're terrified of disappearing.

Taps aff

white as yir unhung laundry
lyin fetit in its baisket

peeliwally bams wi
muckle great Moby Dick kytes

gallus and braw
bletherin oan street coarners

till aboot thir sun-skelpt shooders
the gloamin faws like smirr

as they aye kent it wid

In concert

open yir door an head oot, Sunday moarnin, bind up yir knees, pack thi Ralgex an hink back tae when yir face wiz mair pockparked than thi pitch – ye follow thi whisps ae dreams ye hud as laddies: stadiums full ae cheerin, a crowd watching yi even tho thi reality wiz: ye wir shite – feelin soary fur thi last wan picked but glad yir no it an kennin ye widnae pick 'im eithir – thi fantasy an thi plan B edukashun programme 'learn a trade' – it's no aboot bein a glory hunter, it's aboot faemly, winnin thigithir, thi buzz thi hope – winnin tha Cup wiz thi best hing ah evir did: pride an yir deid da oer yir shooder – aye wantae impress, awbdy ribbin ye if yi dinnae – when yir wee its aw aboot winnin, noo it's thi cameraderie, thi banter wi thi bois, runnin jokes – gettin intae scraps, baw bouncing in tanglt limbs an flyin turf, thi warmth in thi cauld, breath condensin – smile when yi mind wance, when yi wur hungo'er, probably still pished, yi bicycle-kicked thi baw past thi goalie like Maradona an spent thi rist ae thi week flat oan thi flair wi yir back – beer an bovril an squidgy pies – butt slappin towel flickin guid auld heterosexual fun – hidin yirsel, findin yirsel in thi team an breakin free intae thi glory ae space an a wide open goal – play fir thi luv ae thi gayme, thi luv ae each uthir, thi luv ae winnin – line up, shake hauns, shake hauns, shake hauns close thi door – ye injur yirsel an it's guttin cuz ye huvnae gote tha escape oany mair – emty field, naibdy's watchin, naebdy's cheerin – ye've oanly gote lassies an thir no interestet an ye miss whit ye hud wi yir ain faithir, ken ye'll niver huv that – bluebells an shamrocks urnae plants, thur tattoos drawn in blood – bone deep loathin at thi danger anuthur tribe brings, even tho yir no that kindae fan – sum boiys live so oan thi edge a team win's thi only hope thi kin hold oantae an a loss sends thim oer intae violence – hitters gitters – mindin when ye wur wee thir wur aye places ye didnae want thi baw tae bounce: roads, swamps an gairdens wi auld scunners an knives – graiss ripped up by studs – peltit wi rain, plaisters oan yir nips, shins slaeshed by ring-pils – an auld man pickin up glaess an dug shite so ye kin play – stink ae unwashed boadies – ligs blue wi cauld an ye get hit by a baw in thi thigh – ooya! – changin room damp an fetid wi sweat an hot breath – play fir thi fear tha wan day it'll aw huvtae stop – crunch time noo means thi crunch ae cartilage an yir hopes crushed like an empty tin ae Tennents, bitter dregs dripping – rip Velcro, pull ff yir knee brace, limp aff thi field – thi game goes oan wi-oot yi – every chorus fades – dust motes in late summer sun – line up, shake hauns, shake hauns, shake hauns

Scream if you wantae go faster

Lyin still wi sun-scorched
sunlice-ticklt skin, sweat swicked
awa by a gallus breeze
sunk intae gress by yir ain weight,
dae ye evir haud oan tae the surface
ae this earth an feel it spin
sixteen hunnerd mile an oor?

Dae ye evir cling tae the planet:
hook yirsel oan wi yir heels
an shoodir blades, grip
wi yir fingertips, neck tensed, hair fleein,
an hurtle, a thoosan mile a minit
aroon tha collosal baw a blindin origin

fire that warms ye
thit gies blackbirds licence
tae warble and gulls the means
tae drift above ye
in yon deep endless blue

Teacups

The time will come   when we can
            cry again,
                        when a thorn   pierces
                                    surface tension

scatters   what   skates   across   its   surface,

      bleeds it,   mosquito light,
                  drop   by   drop
                  of vacuum-held   starlight.

                        We could

be happy, contained by that same circular
      gravity   that holds back
                              the universe
                  gentle   as a moth wing
                                          holds air.

Palette

    ruined church dry   glacial glen tunnel
      brushed rubble   a cloud ceiling dawn
        fir lined walls   watercolour

   no spirit-stretching   fully framed gilt
       ocean horizon   bronze bracken
          this body   boulder bloom

       deep enough   giggles bounce
   out of your depth   shiny round
     not deep deep   skipping pebbles

    meniscus gravity   siren song
     surface tension   flash of white
      pulling us all in   teeth join us

    under the ripples   ghosts glitter
   shadows lie dark as   fish scale slippery
 the inside of coffins   ungrippable

    pocket a pebble   think I'll turn
 return it take no thing   back are you
      leave nothing   how far are we

     gauge the cold   drip the pat of egg
    with the bobbing   yolk red sauce bacon
   of a rubber duck   grease smears path

parchment dry leaf
litter sun creeping
amber varnish

seal soft silhouettes
plump with tight
contained warmth

white plaster busts
head and shoulders
bob churning halo

dabble numbness
seeping up ankles
stops you dead

a scorpion
hitches a ride
on a frog's back

rust dappled purple
skin keep your
centre warm

water dries on
their canvas
colours fade

no sand underfoot
the universe in
each grain of grit

jump in splash
squeals half frozen
in their rib cages

neoprene armour
hypothermia
nips fingertips

sudden ledge drop
forbidden don't
heart-stop don't

memories sink
spring stippled
edges waves

rough towelling
steam rises
tendrils from flasks

the depths
are here
I'm floating

Mountain Rescue

How do we pull ourselves back
when we've nothing to hold on to?

Find a way clear
or stay? Wait.

Song will arrive again
from scrub, from burn, from leaf.

We feel the weight of hope,
are shocked to life by the rawness of spring-water,
by moonlight on stepping stones
beneath the wildness that rushes,
under rotting bridges,
beyond the rusting fences and crumbling walls
that stand against beating wind, cracking ice
and our dry, splintering sun. Be mindful

of where others have fallen, where snarls
of heather snag ankles, where mud connives
to bind us static. Thorns of gorse pierce
the air and the skitter of scree threatens.

Hold warmth, stick by stick,
in the fires we huddle round.

Where my roots lie

Three trees minded us
while we burned wood.

When day was light
and night was dark
and the world was an amber sphere.

Laughter bounced off the trunks
settled like dusk, like early leaf-fall.
We were one month out of summer
and acrid when we went inside,
rank and blissful with wickedness.

We shinnied up our streetlamp, scaled the wall
into the building site across the road. We ignored
the rats. The boys pissed down the pipes.

Skeletal beams had begun to crisscross my sunsets
so I made my own from their offcuts.
Solid bricks of wood, labelled and stamped,
burned magic, glowing
oil-shimmer auroras that reminded
me of Bunsen burners, fizzing sodium,
comparing tapers and peanuts.

Fire's what happens when anything
gets too much.
It breaks free.

Be careful not to suffocate
a spark before it begins.
Like children, fire needs air.
We construct ourselves daily
turn everything to fate.
Branch-shadows quiver.

My companions grew bored and went off like lost boys
forgetting our parents were only
up and down the road.
A potato lay abandoned, an asteroid
baked to black with a tinfoil tail.

The sky, framed by fir and sycamore
held more than I could fathom.
The moon reflected day
from the other side of the world.
Such a thing, this sense of awe and loneliness.

I rose with warm drafts to drift in the slow
moving sky, entranced by the savagery of it all
held by the blushing, copper-edged embers
cackling ancient tales of caves and handprints
when fire wasn't just for lovers.
When fire was the only thing that stopped us
merging with the darkness. It costs us all
it wants. Leaves nothing but
powdery dark.

Then the rain.

At first the shivering of leaves
made my ears sing with need
I cast my eyes down.
Seeing gets in the way
of the echo inside you.

It was a time I felt alive
waiting for one last perfect flame
when the night was full
and my heart was wild.

Three trees.
At the heartspace between
a fire.

Bonfires
aifter William Blake's 'Auguries ae Innocence'

Ah want tae see the wurld in a grain ae grit
an hivvin in a weed
reflect aw-thing in a gob ae spit
aw time in the growth ae need.

But whit tae dae when aw ye see
ur signs ae oor sad age?
This bee crawlin oan the pavement,
that canary in a cage?

Plaistic poke-bag jellyfish floatin in thi sea.
Peeliewallie maggots stoatin in oor bins.
Polystyrene popcorn nibblt by thi rats,
stappit fu an swollen, stranglt by oor sins.

Stomp a flee an stairve a spider
dugs howlin at thi gates
ae them who tak gold tackity bits
tae this ruin ae a State.

Homeless folk an doves an midgies
boy soajirs droont in oil
laid against each muckle pyre
o common workers' toil.

We woke up this braw bricht moarnin
tae tips in aw oor roads
an naebdy kin get tae work
tae burn on altars tae oor Goads.

Ghost apples

> The earth tips into
> the cold. We slip from
> ourselves, leaving behind
> black-limbed orchards of empty
> peace. Still, all we want
> is to return to normal,
> forget

>> we were never
>> good at leaving. Our
>> seeds spread like the casting
>> of runes. Stay still long
>> enough and we

> slip, speeding
> towards a wild peace
> we're sure we've felt before.
> Normal is just playing
> the same

>> empty song, no
>> upper or lower notes just
>> the black hum of earth.
>> What are we doing
>> anyway, hanging

> around in this
> cold till we forget
> we were ever
> real.

Big John, Dhanakosa, 2014

I sit cross-legged and observe a memory:
two people on a bench in a garden
searching for words.
There are some things it's easier to talk about with strangers.

> *If there's one thing you must do,*
> *kayak on the west coast of Scotland.*
> Big John has a full-bearded,
> thunder-roll of a voice, Yorkshire deep.

She opens her mouth. Closes it again.

> *Go on,* he says.

Why aren't you with your wife and family?

> *I've looked after them all their lives.*
> *I can't carry the weight of the grief in their eyes.*

> His eyes follow the dip and wheel of swallows
> gathering the last of the summer.
> *And why aren't you with your husband?*

She smiles.
The air around them glows in dawn and dusk.
The foulness of his magnificent belly.
Hers tentatively swelling, her silhouette softening.
A midgie cloud phantasm murmurs under the pine trees.

> Every evening after dinner,
> Big John lumbers away into his campervan.

> He keeps his pills there
> *I don't want anyone's pity.*
> and the dusky stink of decay.
> *They tell you to open up a dialogue with what's hurting.*

And have you?

> *We're getting there.* He pats his stomach.

And what's it been telling you?

> *That I should've treated myself with more care.*

With what you ate?

> *What's life without a few bacon butties?*

It's only female midgies that bite.
They're pregnant. It's a kindness not to swat them.
She scratches a red bump on her knuckle.

> *Ulcers and abscesses.*
> *I've spent too long being angry at people.*
> He brushes suffering aside with a casual swipe.
> *This is the most I've lived my life.*

They breathe together
memories like pipe smoke.

> When Big John left,
> his campervan trundled northwards.

Her slow-beating heart

She watches us from her ancient perspectives
pooled in a valley between river and hills.
If we blanket her in paper and scuff a pencil
she might reveal the moments of relief that mark history
the unwritten time that leaves our books bare
as her seabed curves.

Rain whispers in her ear of times when more than water
rolled down her cobbled shoulders.
When we glazed her cleavage
in sewer reek and butcher blood.
How we repaid the protection of her wolves
who howled their warning.
We used her stone to shield our children
from those who'd roughly woo them.
But with walls came containment and we forgot her.

Castles are grand in peacetime, but they're built for war.
When the waters rose we scrambled like fleas to her crown.
Royals and regiments came and left.
We made a battleground of her gardens, grew
shadow puppets and stone-lipped monuments.
In her lap we made a crossroads, built a bridge for goods and Gods.

Winds carve her bones with their own songs of change.
Glaciers and sharpened metal pass over her and recede.
For the hardships she's bided
she's all the more beautiful.
She saves her gifts for those who stay.

Where she swells to the sky, we might lie
with the bees in the plushness of moss and heather
the coiling ebb and flow of the Forth
the mingling of tide and hill water
quicksilver clean, silt-thick fertile and ozone salt
slivers of sun strike and cloud shadow on the carse.
Her deep eyes reflect the sky's seasons
the waxing and waning of the moon
the falling of old nights
the dawning of new days,
memories of fire.

She has no angels to sing of her
only her daughters, her sons:
born of strife, hardened by history
softened by the pulsing of air on her fields
awed by her slow-beating heart.

Flight

grass brushes salt
                          bleached fenceposts scratch   cloud
          shadows stretch to the horizon
                    we bury our dead on the breeze
                        they join runnels of sand
                          streaming
                                to where land meets sea
the more you watch the more you know
              all we are is light
                              from stars long gone
                    carried through
    skies
          in the bellies
              of gulls
old souls
    lapped
              by saltwater tides

Over the edge of blue

A girl sits in a sandy hollow.
Marram grass tickles her neck.
The shadows of dog walkers stretch
long into winter. The tide
calls. She thinks of those brought
by the promise of silver-tipped scales
into faithful embrace. The gasp
of souls lost in a breaking wave.
Pebbles roll with the old bones of a man.

    'Have you ever seen so much sky?'

Years ago, her mother peered
through the hole in the head of a key
in candlelight, the shimmer
of fountain mist to a reflection
of longing. She let her eyes
adjust to the future, the promise
of distant shores, footprints
filled with ozone, widening
over millennia to swallow the risen sea,
crumbling into the infinite.

    'Have you ever seen so much sky?'

Seagulls drift above the memory
of endless summer.
With the push-pull of wind and cirrus,
blue waits, as it does, for the air
to clear, for rain to fall and whisper
welcome. She lifts her eyes to the horizon.

    'Have you ever seen so much sky?'

Thanks

To the Stirling people, our invaluable librarians at Stirling Libraries and Archives, Kate Hudson and Crawford Bell, Fiona McLean, Tara McGloughlin, Mark Lough, Provost Elaine Watterson, Fraser Sinclair, The Book Nook (Stirling), the Curly Coo, Janie and the Stirling Photography Festival, Scene Stirling, Creative Stirling, The University of Stirling's Alumni department and Art Collection team, The Scottish Poetry Library, The Scottish Book Trust, The Federation of Writers (Scotland), GoForth Stirling, Falkirk Writers' Circle, The Macrobert, Curious Seed, Scottish Youth Parliament, StartUp Stirling, my wee Makar feedback group, the Burgh Poets, Sheila Wakefield, fellow Squirrels, Duncan and Charlie at Stewed Rhubarb... and trusted friends, fellow Makars, and family

– for your trust, inspiration, friendship, patience, and giggles,
I offer my deepest gratitude. Your limitless stories
and kindnesses have meant the world
to me over the last four years.

Particular thanks are due to the Civic Panel of Stirling Council for your advice and encouragement throughout my term as Makar, and for your support in producing this publication.

blue

Stewed Rhubarb is Charlie Roy and
Duncan Lockerbie. We are a small, inclusive
press that champions new, diverse poetry.

www.stewedrhubarb.org